SHOP WINDOWS

Cosmetics

SHOP WINDOWS

Cosmetics

arco
editorial

AUTHOR
Francisco Asensio Cerver

EDITOR IN CHIEF
Paco Asensio

PROJECT COORDINATOR
Iván Bercedo (Architect)

PROOFREADING & TRANSLATION
ABC Traduccions

GRAPHIC DESIGN
Mireia Casanovas Soley

LAYOUT
Juan Prieto

Copyright © 1996 Arco Editorial SA
ISBN: 2-88046-283-5

Published and distribution by ROTOVISION SA
Sheridan House
112-116A Western Road
Hove, East Sussex BN3 1DD
England
Tel. 1273 72 72 68
Fax 1273 72 72 69

Production and color separation in Singapore by
ProVision Pte. Ltd.
Tel: (065) 334-7720
Fax: (065) 334-7721

In the complex world of business, dominated in our consumer society by competition and differentiation, the direct sale of a product is always channelled through the shop window. Any commercial enterprise, however small or insignificant it may seem, must, above all other objectives, obtain immediate sales through the scrupulous arrangement of the articles in the shop window. Without doubt they act as the soul of the shop, while at the same time transmitting the personal philosophy of the establishment.

The fashionable shop window of perfumes and cosmetics are directed at a middle- upper class public who have their basic needs well covered and who enjoy a sufficiently refined cultural level. Faced with this factor it is necessary to create a story or develop an exhibition theme that connects with the user and manages to channel the attention in a favourable manner. In other words, it is necessary to create a new type of work of art through the shop window, characterized by the ephemeral and the surprising, which contribute not only to contextualizing the product, but also to embellishing the image of the enterprise, improving the general appearance of the city in which the shop is located.

The concept of coherence, when applied to the overall image of the shop and specifically to the setting out of the display cases, is a quality that contributes to informing the customer about the product on offer and its use. In the opposite case, a lack of unity introduces an ambiguous and disconcerting factor that often leads to mistakes, complicates the comprehension of the display philosophy and nullifies the promotional effort and creative imagination.

Therefore, the projection of the shop window obeys a visual argument in a contextual sense, closely conditioned by the type of product being promoted and the public it is aimed at. Furthermore, this is all subjected to certain physical characteristics. In this sense then, it is always necessary to remember that the shop window is a stage, and as such the space can be manipulated by stands and accessories, always based on the aesthetic imperatives of each season.

Many proposals and solutions are offered in this volume to corroborate these affirmations. The reader interested in the layout of display tableaux, as well as the professional and general public, will understand perfectly the value of coherence, unity and order while also finding surprising and varied solutions adaptable to their own business and which will undoubtedly strengthen creativity and lead to even more possibilities, fruit of the recasting of the various suggestions contained in the book.

Cosmetics

Andrée Putman

▲ The Carita beauty salon is located in
Faubourg Saint-Honoré, a prestigious
commercial area of Paris, where the
most important fashion houses are also
to be found. (A1).

▶ On the following page, the access
stairway to the first floor. The wall
facings, clad with light-coloured wood,
succeed in the creation of a warm and
comfortable atmosphere. (A2)

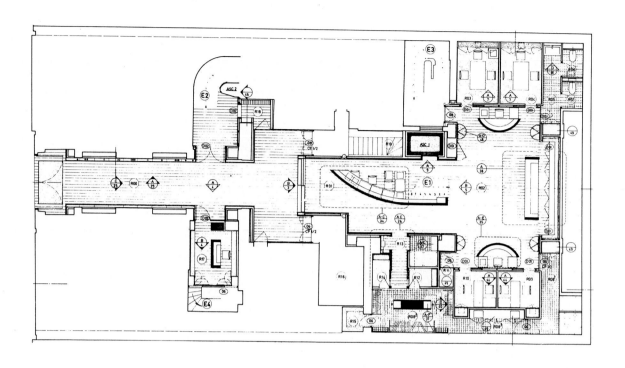

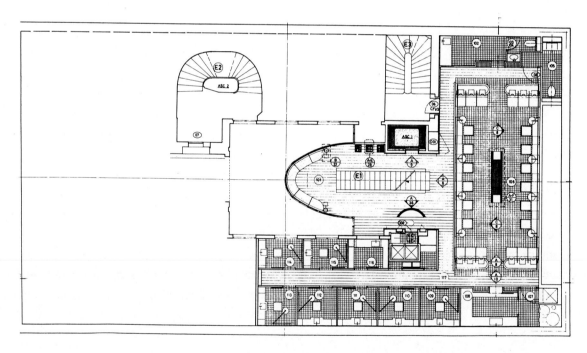

▲ Plans of the ground floor, corresponding to the reception, diagnosis and products sales area (above), the first floor set aside for capillary treatments (below), and the second floor which is given over to the hairdresser's and beauty services (on the following page).

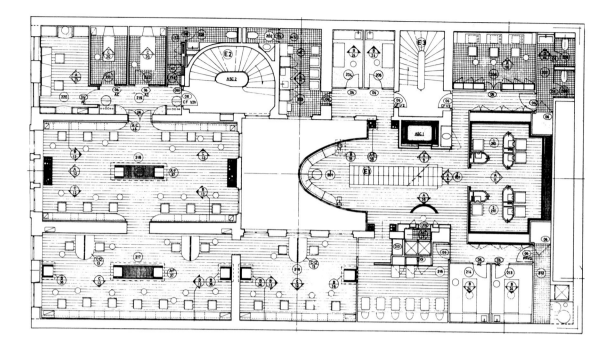

The beauty salon Carita can be found in Faubourg Saint-Honoré, one of the most prestigious commercial areas of Paris, and home to the most famous and distinguished international firms.

What began life as a hairdresser's shop, run by María and Rosy Carita, was gradually extended until at the present time it has come to occupy various floors, and to be considered as one of the most important international beauty salons in terms of quality of service.

Andrée Putman, from the Écart Studio, in collaboration with Bruno Moinard, was entrusted with the project for the latest renovation of the Carita beauty salon.

Carita was conceived of as more of a personal attention service than a commercial sales establishment, strictly speaking. The majority of Carita's customers already know the salon well, or have been well informed about the services which are on offer. As a result, the establishment is hardly in need of promotional elements to capture the attention of passers-by. It is only after the customer has entered the premises that Carita begins to display the range of its products. For this reason the window displays, where Carita's exclusive products are exhibited, are located in the corridor which leads to the salon, once having crossed the threshold and entered into the shop itself. In the form of specially built-in, internally lit, linear showcases, they occupy a narrow eye-level strip, sandwiched between dark grey panels, thus allowing the exhibited products to stand out in stark contrast to the homogeneous background.

Carita occupies the ground floor and three thematically distributed upper floors. The reception is on the ground floor, where the customers are attended and personally directed to the different salons on arrival, there is also a diagnosis booth, which allows for a precise evaluation of the skin in order to discover the precise treatment needed; the Christophe

▶ On the following page a view of the central communications space, conceived as a meeting place for regular customers. This space is dominated by the cool elegance of the metallic planes and lines, in contrast to the warmth of the wood finishes of the upper level and the diaphanous luminosity originating from the overhead skylight.

◀ Below, the area dedicated to the sale of the exclusive range of Carita beauty products (A3). The detailed images above illustrate the structural design of the display counter, in wood, metal and glass; and the continuous plane of wood from which the glass shelving is hung.

▲ The window displays are located in the
passage leading to the salons. Only a
narrow eye-level strip is mounted as a
display case. Crystal paste has been used,
the choice of colour being a neutral grey
tone, which serves as a contrast to the
bright colouring of the articles on display.

Carita studio, in which new models are created; the point of sales for the exclusive product range; a room where videos are shown; the dressing room and the cash register.

The first floor is dedicated to capillary treatments; while the hairdresser's, including all the usual services, manicure, depilation, etc., occupies the second floor.

The third floor is divided between a women's beauty area and another dedicated to men.

The designers have chosen an overall design based on neutral finishes, a peaceful and elegant ambience, bereft of elements which are excessively innovative, and which would only represent an intrusion for the visitors or which could easily become dated in a short period of time. Above all the attempt has been made to render the space comfortable, ensuring that the customers feel relaxed and at their ease.

▲ *The lighting effect for most of the spaces is achieved by means of either indirect light, or light which is screened through glass diffusers. In this way the quality of the ambience is reinforced in the sales areas, bestowing a leading role on the products and emphasising the quality and neutrality of the materials used on this first level (A3).*

▶ *On the following page, one of the spaces of the beauty salon on the second floor. In this area the design is much cooler and more aseptic, relating to the functionality for which it was designed. The great profusion of mirrors acts as a kaleidoscopic extension to the space and has an impressive aesthetic effect.*

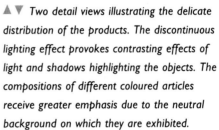

▲ ▼ Two detail views illustrating the delicate distribution of the products. The discontinuous lighting effect provokes contrasting effects of light and shadows highlighting the objects. The compositions of different coloured articles receive greater emphasis due to the neutral background on which they are exhibited.

The stairway is the heart of the establishment. It is not only the main communication element between the different ambiences of the beauty salon, but also constitutes a central space around which the whole establishment is organised. It also allows the regular customers of Carita a place where they can meet up with each other in an atmosphere that is relaxing and pleasant. It was for this very reason that André Putman took particular pains to ensure that it would be a charming and elegant space. The fine quality of the materials used, the meticulous finishes and the natural lighting effect from the overhead skylight have successfully achieved the transmission of this balmy atmosphere.

The beauty salons, in contrast to the hallway and the communal spaces, are clad in ceramic stoneware tiles, in a variety of tones of grey. In these spaces the idea is not to transmit a warm atmosphere, out one that is clean and aseptic, although it maintains the comfort which is characteristic of the entire establishment. ▪

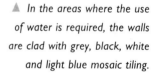 In the areas where the use
of water is required, the walls
are clad with grey, black, white
and light blue mosaic tiling.

◀ *Below, a perspective of the
salon dedicated to masculine
beauty, on the third floor.*

21

LANCÔME

Jacqueume et Henri Boiffils

▲ *The window display, beside the entrance and based on white-veined grey marble elements, introduces the visitor to the symmetrical forms which predominate in the stripped down structural austerity of the establishment. The strategic disposition of the products reinforces the idea of elegant austerity.*

▶ *The display cases are designed to exhibit the products as if they were valuable jewellery or museum pieces. This magnificent marble column serves as both a structural and an aesthetic element, acting as a counterpoint to the voluptuous sinuosity of the stairway, finished in a darker tone of imitation marble.*

◀ *The composition is based on a rigorous symmetry. The entrance is located between the two window display spaces. A white central column defines the semicircular entrance way, delimited by two stylised brass columns. The window displays are sparsely populated, a few products, a photograph of the model who represents the house, sobriety and luxury.*

▶ *Some of the flasks are exhibited in luxurious display cases mounted on marble pedestals. In this case the marbled pedestal is structurally linked to one of the display counters, creating an attractive design.*

From the moment of its creation the prestigious perfumery and cosmetics firm Lancôme, has been located at number 29 Faubourg Saint-Honoré, in the centre of Paris.

The renovation work carried out by Jacqueline and Henri Boiffils, as well as effecting a thorough modernisation of the premises, also gave expression to the elegance which has always been associated with the name of Lancôme. The most noble materials were used in combinations of elegant austerity

▼ *The carpet which occupies the centre of the floor space confers a sense of movement and vitality in juxtaposition to the inherent coolness of the marble.*

with a reliance on minimal resources and the introduction of a variety of classical references.

The decoration is limited to the flasks and bottles of perfumes, and the cosmetics products, exhibited here almost as if they were jewellery, and the sumptuousness of the furnishings and finishes. It is precisely the use of certain selected materials, such as marble, brass and glass, allied to the absence of ornamental elements, which contributes to the atmosphere of aseptic luxury with which Lancôme wanted to imbue this combined shop and institute of beauty.

The representative signals are already evident on the façade itself, with the employment of the materials and the colours which distinguish the house of Lancôme. The white marble columns, the grey marble of the flooring, the brass of the structural work and the expansive planes of glass, are all present.

▼ *Both the occasional shelf built-in to the wall, and also those incorporated as part of the furnishings, are made up of surprisingly thick sheets of plate glass. A few products are displayed on these shelves, emphasising their luxurious and exquisite characteristics.*

▶ *On the following page, a detail view of the stepped glass shelving in the form of a pyramid.*

The three colours which define the brand are included here: grey, white and gold.

The composition is based on a rigid symmetry, where the entrance is located between the two display window spaces, a centrally located white column defines the semicircular space of the entrance doorway, which is framed by two stylised brass columns. The window displays are characterised by a minimal presence of products and a large format portrait photograph of the model who represents the company, the juxtaposition of sobriety and luxury.

The premises occupy two floors. On the ground floor the white marble columns are interspersed with pedestals in grey marble, which support display cases, in a variety of forms and containing a few flasks of Lancôme perfume.

Two beauty booths are located on this floor, the atmosphere is warmer, the walls are clad with mottled maple panel-work, picked out with leather, steel or brass decorative finishes. ■

▼ *The sobriety and luxury which are so characteristic of the company are reflected in the precise and exquisite layout of the exhibited products, and also in the serene beauty of the image of the Lancôme model. The greatest possible attention to detail is a primordial characteristic of the window dressing technique in these premises.*

▶ *The lighting, based on spots built into the ceiling, has been treated as a mere form of underlining the atmosphere. In the display panels and cases, on the other hand, its function is more defined, contributing to the highlighting of the image of the products*

ALFREDO CARAL

Angel Sánchez Bernuy

▲ The colours of the flasks and containers of the
products creating a warm and pleasant atmosphere
has been one of the primordial objectives behind the
design of Ángel Sánchez Bernuy, where the smallest
detail is required to be representative of the overall
design of the premises.

▶ On the following page, a detail of one
of the side display counters, the attractive design
of which is perfectly integrated into the
atmospheric concept of the shop. The ochre and
brown tones of the wood and the marble reinforce
the aesthetic quality of Alfredo Caral (1).

◄ *The entrance to the premises is through a pedestrian precinct. The façade has been resolved with great simplicity. From outside the shop we have a complete vision of the interior of the perfumery, due to a continuous floor to ceiling plate glass wall and a half height display element which respects the view of the passers-by in the street (3).*

▼ *A view from the entrance of the semicircular apse in the background, also illustrating the individual cylindrical chests of drawers, finished in peanut coloured formica, and completely integrated in the colour scheme which dominates the design of the premises (2).*

► *The premises are of a strictly symmetrical composition. The floor plan, dominated by the semicircular apse, in an evocation of a temple dedicated, in this instance, to commerce*

The Alfredo Caral perfumery occupies a site on the ground floor of the Hotel Palace, at number 39, Galería del Prado, in Madrid. The hotel building was built in 1912 in a Neo-Baroque style and is situated in a privileged environment, next to the Plaza de Neptuno and near the Palacio de las Cortes Españolas and the Palacio de Villahermosa, in which the Thyssen collection of paintings is exhibited.

Working on the basis of premises with a trapezium shaped floor plan, some five metres wide and eight and a half metres long, the architect Ángel Sánchez-Bernuy decided to incorporate a semicircular apse directly in front of the oblique back wall of the premises, leaving room for a small storage area in the dead space behind the curved back wall.

The façade of the pedestrian precinct has been resolved by simply installing a floor to ceiling glass wall, with an inset doorway, along the length of this frontage. The name of the perfumery is written in dark lettering on the glass itself.

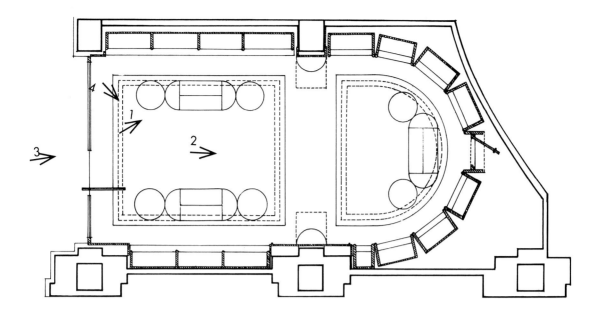

The ceiling of the shop was given a stepped design, with a white antique plaster finish, and houses the air conditioning shafts, it also serves to disguise a concrete structural beam, which runs across the width of the premises.

All of the wall space is occupied by shelving with light coloured wooden uprights and adjustable glass shelves which are backed by mirror facings. Below each of these shelving modules, there are double columns of drawers with cut glass handles.

Three display counters have been installed, one at each side, and a third at the back of the shop. They consist of a central unit, with two glass shelves and semicircular elements at both ends, finished with peanut coloured formica.

On each side of the display counters a cylindrical chest of drawers has been placed, finished in the same material.

The flooring is of flags of polished Travertino marble, 40 cm. by 60 cm., with two central strips, dividing the rectangular space of the semicircular apse, and a perimeter of black Portoro marble.

The furnishings and the finishes, in a certain way, act as a reminder of the atmosphere of the Hotel Palace itself, dominated by warm tonalities, not only in terms of the materials chosen, but also through the colours of the containers of the products on display, almost all of which are packaged in red and ochre tones. ▨

◄ ▲ *The counters and the chests of drawers are finished with peanut coloured formica. The non-exclusive character of the shop justifies the seemingly disordered yet elegant display of products. The independent counters help to individualise some of the different brands on offer. (4)*

◄ *The products are arranged basically more in terms of harmony than contrast. The strategic disposition of some jewellery items emphasise a selection of the shops most important products.*

► *This front view of the interior of the premises illustrates some of its principal characteristics: the perfect symmetry which dominates the layout, the magnificent spatial juxtaposition of the semicircular apse, and the stepped design of the white plaster ceiling.*

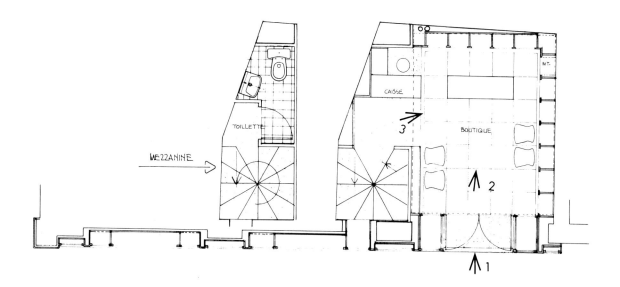

▲ *Floor plans of the main level and the small upper floor. The apparent symmetry of the premises is achieved by reserving the principal rectangular space for the sales and display area, and grouping the less representative services together at the side: till, stairs and washrooms.*

◄ *A detail view of one of the niches in the façade. The dominant colours are the same as those found inside the perfumery, ivory, pastel, jade and golden tones. The motifs chosen for the ornamentation of the window display, different seashells, also form an integral part of the overall look.*

The Annick Goutal perfumery is situated in Rue de Castiglione, a porticoed street in the centre of Paris.

Although the premises are relatively small, the corresponding facade is much bigger. As well as the exterior of the establishment, it takes in another relatively long section of the building's facade which is also exploited as a display window surface. As a result the impression of the perfumery from the street is of a much larger establishment than it is in reality.

The modulation of the facade is based on an ordering of the different display windows according to the principles of classical styling. Alternating between the three arches, corresponding to two niches and the entrance doorway, are rectangular windows which display samples of some of Annick Goutal's own brand perfumes. The ivory-colour lacquered structural work has been interspersed with designed classical pilasters and mouldings. The window frames and the niches are finished with gold-leaf. The name of the shop is written in gold letters above each

▼ The arches of the façade are picked up again inside the shop. This allows for a full exploitation of the perimeter space. The diaphanous nature of this arched layout is reinforced by a strategic study of the colour scheme, the textures and the diffuse lighting effect (2)

▲ The flasks of perfume are arranged in a rigorous display order. the glass surfaces duplicate the product, creating an attractive optical interplay. The minuscule attention paid to the details is one of the parameters of the design.

◀ ▶ The diffuse lighting creates an ethereal and immaculate atmosphere which blends into the predominant aesthetic concept. The perimeter of the flooring is paved with grey marble, emphasising the verticality of the side arcades (3).

42

of the arches on a black glass surface, providing a stylish juxtaposition, which highlights the brilliance of the sign. The top of the facade is rounded off with a series of lintels, which again bear the name of the shop in relief golden letters. The whole of this facade is profusely lit at night by spots built into the lintels, and also by the light which emanates from the interior through the display and niche windows.

Inside the shop the forms and colours of the facade are consciously repeated The layout of the shop interior is misleadingly symmetrical, one side is occupied by a stairway, which leads up to the wash rooms, and the cash register. It is a matter of a reduced space, in which the only projecting element is the counter.

The shelving units run round the remaining three walls. On each of the glass shelves various units of a single product have been arranged in the form of a wedge. Above the shelving units there are a series of irregular arches, and below, the units are divided into draws and small cupboards finished with white lacquer. As in the facade, gold coloured elements have been arranged as ornaments, knobs, handles, counter rims, shelf brackets and filaments worked into the mouldings of the units. The floor is of cream coloured marble, with a grey marble perimeter. The spots are almost all hidden away behind the mouldings, which results in a diffuse lighting effect. ■

▲ *The golden and ivory tones are not only characteristic of the establishment, but also form part of the design concept of the product packaging.*

▶ *All of those products forming part of a single range of perfumery are disposed on the same display unit.*

ETRO

Eugenio Gerli

▲ A view of the entrance-way seen from
inside the shop. The curtains can be
drawn across to isolate the shop from the
outside world, constituting yet another
element which adds to the suggestion of

► The furnishing of Etro is evidently
inspired by the classical mode and a taste
for traditional aesthetics. The shelving is

◄ The antique elaboration apparatus is a means of attracting the interest of the visitor, not only from a merely aesthetic point of view, but also for the confidence which is imparted by the presence of these gadgets which convey the antiquity of the firm's perfumery tradition.

The design concept introduced to Jean-François Laporte's perfumery, Maître Parfumeur et Gantier, located at number 84 Rue de Granelle in Paris, is the work of Jean Louis Riccardi and is intended to illustrate the great tradition of French perfumery, recreating the atmosphere of the end of the 17th century.

The facade, however, has maintained the compositional balance and the look typical of central Parisian shops. There is a central double door flanked by two large square display windows. The structural framework is of a dark green painted wood, with particularly robust window frames and abundant mouldings. The display windows are vertically marked out by a wooden panel, running the width of the facade and bearing the shop name in gold letters, and below by a base board, also in wood.

The decorative elements which make up the window display, examples of antique apparatus

▲ ▼ The perfumery is housed in a Neo-classical building, characteristic of the city of Paris. The façade respects the typical aesthetics of commercial properties in the area, and from the very entrance way explicit reference is made to the traditional intentions which have formed these premises.

◄ *The interior is dominated by gold, purple and grey tones. A great profusion of natural light also washes in through the large plate glass windows, there is a large lamp in the form of an inverted bell-shape, another reference to traditional ornamentation.*

▼ *Spray and ambience perfumes are other products on offer in this shop. They are exhibited on the splendid individual shelves of three levels, with stylised scrolls and bases draped with red velvet cloths.*

and techniques for the elaboration of perfumes, aim to convey the singularity of this perfumery to the passers-by. As a result the window displays are conceived of more in terms of a theatrical or representative space than for the display of goods for sale.

The design of the interior is dominated by gold and purple tones, and by ornamental elements redolent of the Grand Siècle. The ceilings are decorated with trompe l'oeil paintings, the walls richly covered with damask tapestries, the mouldings intricately worked, the corners are decorated with double pilasters, there are glass fronted display cases built into the walls and lined with purple cloth, and the door jambs and skirting boards are of veined black marble.

The visitor finds himself entering a time tunnel, coming face to face with antique uses and customs, which Jean François Laporte has

▼ *A view from the interior towards the Parisian Rue de Granelle. All of the components reflect a traditional atmosphere: the structure of the container, emphasised by the mouldings and pilasters with Corinthian capitals; and the use of display furnishings and their stylistic debt to the eighteen hundreds.*

► *The variety of fragrances elaborated do not represent a multiplicity of formats.*

► *The workshop is separated from the sales area by a black marble doorway, in which a burgundy coloured drape hangs. The exquisite interior decoration not only affects the sober and elegant materials, but also the colour, schematic and textural combinations which bestow an atmosphere of antiquity on the interior*

◄ *The base of dried aromatic herbs, on which the flasks are displayed, constitutes another of the design elements which make reference to the seriousness and traditional background to the work of the perfumist.*

presented both as a manner of attracting attention and as a seal of quality.

The singular forms of the furnishings also reflects the Rococo age. The three principle display elements consist of stepped shelving units, supported by four exuberant wooden scrolls, placed on top of counters covered with red velvet cloths. A large lamp, in the form of an upturned bell, hanging from the ceiling by burgundy coloured cords, dominates the central space of the shop. Two small trees stand sentry either side of the entrance doorway. The flasks themselves are faithful reproductions of those from the 17th and 18th centuries, and are presented as yet another decorative element in this historically recreated ambience. The dry flowers, from which the products are obtained, can be seen both on the shelves and in the window displays, demonstrating to the visitor this establishment's concern with craftsmanship and traditional practices. ■

▼ *The shelves for the display of the products are a reminder of the exquisite design of the flasks themselves. The stylised forms of the scrolls, which support the shelves, recapture a refined sense of the Rococo age, very much in tune with the overall design of the shop.*

The lamp hanging from the ceiling is one of the central elements of the interior composition. It is a focusing element, which draws the attention of the client towards the profusely adorned ceiling of the premises, featuring trompe l'oeil paintings and a perimeter surround of exquisitely worked mouldings. The structural definition, thus, acts as a complement to the luxurious wealth of the style of the furnishings.

The dried flowers, from which the perfumes are obtained, are also displayed. They constitute an ornamental motif which, together with the exhibition of the ancient instruments of perfumery, symbolise the traditional and conservationist nature of an art which is becoming increasingly industrialised.

CRABTREE & EVELYN

Proper Devas

▲ *A general view of the interior of the shop. The atmosphere created by Prosper Devas is evanescent and subtle, based more on eclecticism than on uniformity, yet thoughtfully combined. The diaphanous play of light and the subtle design and colour scheme of the hand painted wallpaper, on both walls and ceiling, contributes to this effect.*

▶ *The floral motifs, particularly the dried flowers which adorn the corners of the interior, respond to the naturalistic aesthetic. Every aspect has been thought out to the last detail.*

▲ For the location of this French branch the English firm decided to renovate an old bookshop on the Boulevard Saint Germain. The façade, in blue lacquered wood, was conserved for its traditional air. Two large display windows flank the central doorway, dominated by a large sign, in golden letters, and in each of the windows the crab apple trees which are the emblem of the firm.

▼ A frontal view of one of the display window: a small window ledge, bearing the name of the firm, serves as the base for the composition which is framed by blue wood. The window dressing technique demonstrates a respect for the natural visual plane, seen from the street.

The Tree perfumery is located in Calle Ricardo Calvo, in the Bonanova area of Barcelona, one of the most sought after residential areas of the city.

The renovation project was taken on by a team from the Zero Studio, with a great deal of experience in the assessment and design of interiors.

A very successful decision was made to recess the entrance to the shop, thereby increasing the available surface area for display windows and subtly drawing the window shoppers and passers-by off the street and into the shop itself.

Here we find the window displays decorated for the Christmas period. The result is a combination of allusions, both to the character of the shop itself and to the range of products for sale, mostly elaborated on the basis of natural ingredients, also included are the decorative elements and images typical of the season. Various bundles of reeds, tied with blue velvet ribbons, are arranged creating a

▲ *Views of the display window area which leads in towards the interior of the establishment. The door is set back from the plane of street and façade, creating a transitional space which allows for a better appreciation of the products on display in the lateral window displays. In the smaller illustration, a view of the shop's façade, seen from the street.*

▶ *This view of the interior illustrates some of the structural details which contribute to the creation of a certain classicism: the moulded friezes around the perimeter of the ceiling, and the pilasters, toped off with Corinthian styled capitals.*

◄ *Despite the undue length of the floor plan, the intelligent lay out of the display elements give the interior the appearance of width, bathed in a diaphanous and luminous lighting effect. In the lower photograph, one of the antique counters recovered from a turn of the century perfumery, in Anton Gaudí's emblematic "Pedrera", and subsequently restored.*

▼ *The choice of the flooring was one of the most outstanding successes of the interior of the shop. The flooring of quarry tiles, hand fired, is a perfect counterpoint to the selected colour scheme of the walls and the ceiling, reinforced by the lighting effect of the built-in halogen spots*

natural space with a volumetric balance consisting of different levels and unusual perspectives. The bundles are topped off and surrounded with moss, on top of which, as if sitting on cushions, the Christmas ornaments are strewn: bows, small wooden figures, ceramics and even teddy bears, in an arrangement which is lively, amusing and richly colourful.

The interior is dominated by pink tones and earth hues. The floor is of quarry tiles, the walls and the ceiling are sponge painted, simulating pink marble, the columns and the friezes in a darker tone, the wall colouring lighter, and the ceiling painted flat, using a paler colour to give a sense of greater height and spaciousness. In contrast, both the interior and exterior structural framework has been painted navy blue. The shelving units and counters were rescued from an old turn of the century perfumery, originally located in Antoni Gaudí's "Pedrera", in Barcelona. Each article of furnishing has been individually renovated and adapted to the aesthetics of the new premises, with the introduction of subtle changes, such as painting the edges in matching navy blue, or lining the interiors of the display cases with terracotta coloured velvet fabric.

Apart from the display elements recovered from the old perfumery, a few fine glass shelves have also been included allowing for the display of the complete range of products. ▪

▲ A frontal view of one of the lateral display units. As well as the antique wooden counters, the display space has been increased through the use of fine glass shelves which, due to their discretion, do not interrupt the visual perspectives of the interior.

▶ In response to the Christmas shopping season, a window dressing technique has been chosen which takes nothing away from the interior space. The tones and textures of the selected ornamental motifs respect the aesthetic quality of the container.

The mirrors located behind the glass shelves further increase the reflections on the flasks of perfume, thus increasing the sensation of spaciousness and transparency, which contributes to the creation of a subtle and elegant atmosphere.

The smallest possible detail of the arrangement of the products is taken care of with a precision which endows them with a character of exclusivity and distinction. Glass on glass, the flasks stand out as delicate containers of valuable essences.

The Garden Perfumery

◀ *The focal point of the decorative scheme is a tree trunk clad with dried leaves, arranged as a sculpture in the centre of the premises and evoking connotations of autumn. This naturalistic composition, which goes beyond the limits of artistic manifestation, constitutes one of the most spectacular focal points of the shop interior.*

▼ *The sculptural motif of autumnal foliage is repeated in the window displays. The name of the establishment is also outstanding, written on one of the glazed surfaces which make up the façade of the shop, as well as a mask, another of the ornamental motifs, which introduces an ambiguous and mysterious aspect to the atmosphere of the premises.*

The Garden Perfumery is a shop specialising in perfumes, beauty and skin care products, all of which are elaborated on the basis of natural ingredients.

It is located in Floral Street, Covent Garden, one of the most central and exclusive areas of London.

The founder of The Garden Perfumery, Raza Syed, understood that the image of the shop had to reflect a combination of romanticism and a certain sophistication. The particular nature of the products offered by the shop would have to be identifiable through the interior design of the establishment itself, in this way attracting the passers-by of Covent Garden, who Raza Syed saw as the ideal customers for his cosmetics.

The project was finally adjudicated to the designers John Misick and John Newman, of McColl Architecture, an architecture and

interior design company working internationally, with offices in London, New York, Miami and Madrid.

Their project was to give a subtle twist to the logic of Raza Syed's original proposal. The only thing that could truly evoke the spirit of the Garden Perfumery's products were the products themselves. Thus their efforts were exclusively centred on displaying those products in a diaphanous way, converting them into the principal decorative element,

▲ *The display shelves are constructed with light and airy planes, which impose no obstacle to the perception of the interior. In some cases there is a grouping together of the flasks, displayed on hexagonal glass trays, in an attractive interplay of glass on glass.*

◄ *Just behind the glass paneled entrance doors, arranged on two shelves, the flasks are central to the foreground exhibition of the window displays, without obstructing the view of the interior. Through the respect shown for the natural field of vision of the passers-by, emphasis is placed on the commercial finality of the establishment, as the opportunity is made available to fully enjoy the magnificent products which are offered inside the shop.*

to which all other design decisions would be subordinated.

The exterior facade is subdivided into four glazed modules, the furthest to the left of which is the entrance doorway. The exterior finish is of dark green painted wood, this composition reflecting the typical look of English shops, with the shop signs located above the windows.

▲ *These rounded boxes, arranged in the form of a pyramid, and the groups of containers arranged in specific shapes and forms, constitute an added decorative element. This rigorous pyramid shaped composition is counterpointed by the soft pastel tones of the boxes and a juxtaposition to the natural aesthetic of the sculptural tree, which serves as the central leitmotif of the interior design of the premises.*

◀ *This image offers a different perspective of the central motif of the ornamentation of the premises: a combination of the sinuous tree trunk, covered in foliage, and the masks create an almost artistic overall effect, which perfectly conjugates with the exposed brickwork with which the walls are clad.*

93

Just behind the shop windows two shelves, hung from the ceiling by steel cables, allow for the exhibition of flasks of perfume and cosmetics containers in the foreground, yet also allow the passer-by an almost uninterrupted view of the interior.

Special care was taken with the lighting, a combination of low voltage lights and halogen lamps being used generally, and to highlight the products on display.

The shelves and shelving units have been reduced to the simplest minimalist expression, in glass or wood, suspended from the ceiling by wires.

The flasks and containers, on the other hand, are arranged in groups, creating specific forms or illustrating a play of contrasts.

Persian blinds have been hung behind the display windows, which can be lowered to permit a simple variation of the decorative background, reflecting the atmospheric variation of the different seasons.

This exclusive decorative concept was suggested by John Misick himself, allowing the spirit of the products to be brought out and providing them with a personal stamp of freshness, clean lines and an essential refinement. ■

▼ *On this page, one of the corners of the shop, one of the most discreet and elegant areas of the premises. The lighting effect is soft and diffuse, underlining the clarity and sharpness of the cream coloured planes, highlighting the surfaces of the mirror, with its voluptuous curved top edge.*

▶ *On the following page, a close up view of the shelves located just behind the display windows, suspended from the ceiling by steel ropes which allow for the arrangement of products facing the street, without interrupting the visual perspectives from the exterior.*

LOURED, PERFUMED OR ANIMAL TESTED *The Garden Perfumery*

SOTHYS

Jean-Jacques Ory

▲ Each and every corner of the Sothy's Institute of Beauty offers an image of classical sobriety, adorned, in many cases, with plants which introduce a natural counterpoint.

▶ An image of the space set aside for the waiting room, in which the modern designer furnishings are absolutely in tone with the classical serenity which inundates the overall atmosphere.

◀ The façade of Sothy's reflects the distribution on two levels. The exterior treatment differentiates the premises from the building as a whole: the composition is divided into modules, emphasising the name of the shop in relief, and introducing a break from the continuous travertine cladding which characterises the rest of the façade of this building.

▶ A detail of one of the display units. the products are distributed on a base of tiles which imitate a smooth marble finish.

◀ The composition of the window display modules relies on materials which contrast within the overall look of the façade: oxidised brass, framing Stadip plate glass windows, the green tones of which has an eye-catching effect in this Parisian street.

In one of the most luxurious shopping areas of the French capital, at number 128 Rue du Faubourg Saint Honoré, Sothys perfumery and beauty institute can be found.

Located in an old office building, dating from the thirties, the design of the project for the new establishment was the work of the Jean Jaques Ory architectural office, a firm specialising in the renovation of singular buildings. The work was done by a team of collaborators: Jean Ribereau Gayon worked on the architectural aspects, Berengère de Hennin on the interior design, and Christian Lobert acted as the project co-ordinator. The building company Alpha International carried the work out.

The composition of the facade includes both the ground and the first floors. Although the concept expressed an essential respect for the overall style of the building, at the same time the space occupied by Sothys was differentiated, through the variation in the

▲ *A different view of the reception area and the waiting room. The atmosphere of classicism is achieved by means of the subtlety of the colour scheme, the choice of flooring and the strategic location of the imitation marble columns, which have been sliced off just below the level of the capital to introduce a spot, which is directed up towards the ceiling, creating a highly suggestive lighting effect.*

treatment of the materials. The existing travertine of the facade was subjected to an intense cleaning process, oxidised brass was then used for the structural framework, and Stadip window panes were installed. The facade is divided both vertically and horizontally into three modules. The lower module, the ground floor, includes the entrance doorway and the display window, the first floor is divided into two modules, one intermediate, with mirror glass on which the name of the establishment has been mounted in relief, and the upper module, consisting of windows with protective slats.

Inside, a large salon with a classical atmosphere, such as that which could be found in the atrium of Roman bath-houses, serves as both a shop for the firm's own cosmetics products and as a reception for the institute of beauty, which is located the other side of the frosted glass doors.

The finishes have been given a treatment in pinks and creams, in order to generate a placid and pleasant atmosphere. The result comes close to the atmosphere of a garden; an abundance of plants, some of which are exuberant, chairs, benches and tables in strangely shaped white lacquered steel, individually selected to assume the role of one of the principle decorative elements of the salon. In a series of classical imitation marble columns, cut off just below the capital, and

▶ *A detail of one of the corners of the ground floor, which also serves as both a reception area for the Beauty Institute and a sales area for the firm's products. Natural motifs, frosted glass and the presence of the imitation marble columns help to create the relaxed and serene atmosphere desired.*

housing a spot directed upwards towards the capital improbably appended to the ceiling. The overall effect adds further to the sensation of relaxation and serenity.

Pink marble from Portugal was chosen for the flooring, light-coloured wood for the display furnishings, and cream coloured stucco for the wall facings, combined with mirrors behind the glass shelving units which serve as the permanent exhibition space for many of the company's products. The lighting effects underline the clarity and transparency of the materials used. As well as the built-in ceiling spots, the show cases are amply lit by individual lighting panels, the light from which reflects down off the rear mounted mirrors. ■

ANNE SEMONIN

Bernard Magin

▶ All of the surfaces have been
clad with white stoneware tiles, imposing a
homogenous style on the space which is
both clear and diaphanous.

▲ Three shrubs have been placed outside the
shop to mark out the space.

▲ *One of the walls is completely occupied by a mirror which allows for an optical duplication of the space.*

◄ *On the previous page, a detail view of the window display. There is a complete view of the establishment from the exterior.*

Anne Sémonin is located in the Rue de Petits-Champs in Paris, just round the corner from the Place des Victoires. The renovation of these premises, one of several that this company has carried out in the French capital, the wur it/of out by the architect Bernard Magin of the company Bernard Magin, Etudes et Chantiers.

The result is a work of spectacular formal simplicity, almost minimalist, with the use of very few decorative elements to define the space. A constant finish of white stoneware tiles has been used throughout, for the flooring, the walls, the finishing on the counter, the window display and the seating units. The composition of the facade, was decided with the same formal economy as the interior. The only two openings, corresponding to the door and the display window, are defined by monolithic planes of glass, reaching from the floor to the ceiling.

The name of the establishment is inscribed

▲ *The furnishings have been reduced to a bare minimum. Some of the elements are built-in, and have been covered with tiles, creating a homogenous atmosphere with the floor and the walls.*

◄ *A detail of the shelves. The products are arranged according to a geometric order.*

in marble-white letters on a white satin strip above the display window, on a half lowered blind which occupies the upper part of the display window, and on a rectangular tiled panel above the doorway.

The window display area consists of two stepped white stoneware tiled surfaces: the foremost at floor level and a second with a height of some 50 centimetres. A sparse mathematical distribution of products is arranged in this space, accompanied by an advertising photograph and a white varnished table lamp with a shade of the same colour

The interior consists of a small square area. However the option to fully exploit this limited space, with a tumultuous accumulation of objects, has not been taken up. A mere four elements occupy the space: a built-in seat, a counter with two stools, a narrow wooden table, on which is placed an exuberant plant, and a desk. The products are arranged behind the counter on the only shelves in the shop,

and along a step which intervenes between the wall and the floor. The arrangement is in groups of a single product, with a certain distance separating the groups. Opposite the counter, a mirror has been mounted on the door-side wall, which optically duplicates the space and the light. Across the back of the shop an ivory coloured screened wall separates the public space from the workshop.
The lighting comes from spots located in each of the four corners of the premises and pointing upwards towards the ceiling.
Two lines of lighting tubes are also installed underneath the shelves. ■

▶ *The totality of the products on sale are displayed on just two continuous shelves, mounted behind the counter.*

▼ ▶ The aesthetics of the premises are reflected in the containers and the labelling. Bernard Magim combines the white colour of the tiles and the finishing of the shelves with the colour of the recipients and the labels.

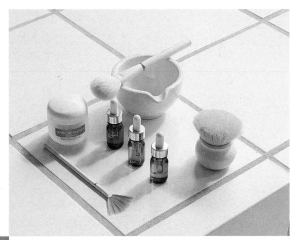

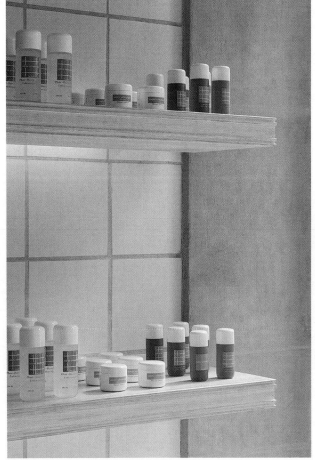

▶ Two plants break up the tonal uniformity of the establishment. A border with geometrical details reminds the old arabic friezes.

BARATTI

Federico Brunetti, Fiorella Montanari

▲ *In the window displays the products are arranged around advertising photographs. A metallic structure defines the back and sides of each window display. (1)*

▶ *A feature of the interior is its great luminosity, not only due to the large arches of the façade, but also due to the materials and colours which were chosen for the finishings. (2)*

▲ A panoramic view of the main entrance. The surface area of the display window has been extended by recessing the doorway itself, in relation to the plane of the street. From this point the various routes for the exploration of the interior are merely suggested by the lines marked out on the flooring, and by certain changes in the composition of the flooring itself. (3)

▼ The image below, illustrates one of the display windows set aside for cosmetic products. The design is modern and functional, distanced from any of the traditional or classical aesthetics that are frequently associated with this kind of establishment. The multi-functionality of the premises demanded a more up to date stylistic treatment. (4)

The Schuerman perfumery is located in an unusual building, it formerly had a religious function, in the centre of the Dutch town of Terneuzen. The premises are a combination of a drugstore, a chemist's and a perfumery. This factor not only increases the number of potential customers, but has also led to the uniting of three different services within a single design concept, the work of Benschop B.V., a Dutch designers collective.

The premises are situated in a privileged, and highly attractive, commercial location, with a layout which is extensive in comparison with other perfumeries, it covers a total surface area of 330 square metres.

The length of the facade also presented a sufficient section of window display space for the Benschop B.V. designers, allowing them

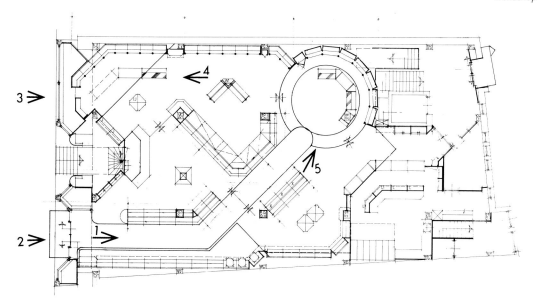

▲ *The complexity of this floor plan is an accurate reflection of the multi-functionality of these extensive premises, some 330 square metres. The establishment has various entrances which allow for a certain unrestricted and natural freedom of circulation around the interior. All of these different routes are centred on a great circular surface area, set aside for the display of cosmetics products.*

to develop a dislocated play of forms, of recesses and projections, conforming angular spaces in which eye-catching display combinations are arranged against a diffuse and continuous cream coloured backdrop.

At the same time, both the typology of the lettering and the design of the perfumery's shop signs transmit an image that is at once direct and uncomplicated. The entrance doorway is somewhat recessed in relation to the plane of the facade.

A series of circuits have been traced out between the product display shelving units, inside the shop. A subtle variation in the design concept is evident, according to the service concerned, be it perfumery, drugstore or chemist's. This works as an incentive to self service shopping in certain sectors, yet is staff centred in others. The chemist's sector is marked out by a change in the flooring. The perfumery and cosmetics sector is clearly indicated by an enormous circular lighting module, suspended from the ceiling, as well as the grey fitted carpet, in marked contrast to the uniform travertine flooring of the premises in general.

It is an atmosphere in which grey and white tones predominate, which is relaxing, quiet and efficient. The rigorous ordering and modulation of the shelving units not only enables the customer to find the products with ease, and without the need to ask a sales assistant, it also contributes to the general sensation of efficiency. The ceiling is of plaster panels, installed along obliquely angled lines and accentuating the dynamism of the premises. The designers renounced the possibility of creating a luxurious space, concentrating instead on a clean functionality the result of which is possibly more attractive. ▪

▼ *In this image we can see the circular space set aside for the display and sale of cosmetics products. The great overhead lighting module is outstanding, and converts this into the most representative space within the complex. the discreet and functional counter, is fitted to the circular perimeter of the space, featuring suggestive angles.*

▶ *The photograph on the following page, illustrates one of the individual display modules from the circular perfumery and cosmetics area. It is designed around two columns with slots which allow the shelves to be fitted at different heights.*

◄ The photographs on this page, show two images of the space set aside for cosmetics. the choice of the grey carpet, to cover the floor, contributes a differentiating factor with regard to the rest of the spaces. Both the shelf lighting, and also the built-in spots, contribute to the creation of a modern, yet comfortable, atmosphere.

► This image illustrates a detail of the arrangement of the products in one of the window displays. The different brands are grouped together in distinct sections, not rigidly but in a continuous and natural way. The soft cream tonalities of the background also contribute to this effect.

▲ A detail view of a selection of the products displayed in the shop window. The articles for sale are playfully interspersed with objects unconnected with the world of cosmetics, such as toy cars, offering an eye-catching juxtaposition. (1)

► On the following page, a view of the interior through the double entrance doors. The façade is divided into vertical modules, one of which serves as the double doorway, allowing access to the establishment.

The Body Shop chain, with establishments in many of Europe's most important cities, has succeeded in creating a recognisable and characteristic aesthetic. The Vienna branch of this international chain can be found on the populous Mariahifer Strasse, one of the busiest commercial areas of the Austrian capital.

On this occasion the architect in charge of the conversion of these old premises, which had been first opened in the fifties, was Hans Peter Sockel, who succeeded in adapting them to the aesthetics and the spirit of The Body Shop. The first priority which he set himself for this project was the liberation of the interior, removing the existing partition walls in order to achieve a single, more extensive, open plan space.

The old steel doorway was substituted for one of dark green lacquered wood, the same

▲ *A detail of one of the window displays. The products are arranged in geometric groupings made up of containers of the same article. The parcelled boxes are used as props, on top of which the products are then placed.*

▼ *A panoramic view of the façade. The composition is based on a traditional aesthetic. The enormous lit shop sign not only unifies the whole but also, because of its size and the effect of the direct lighting, emerges as one of the most outstanding visual elements in the street.*

► *On the following page, a detail view of one of the shelving units, fully stacked with products. The basic colours: red, green and yellow, are used to endow the overall effect with greater vivacity.*

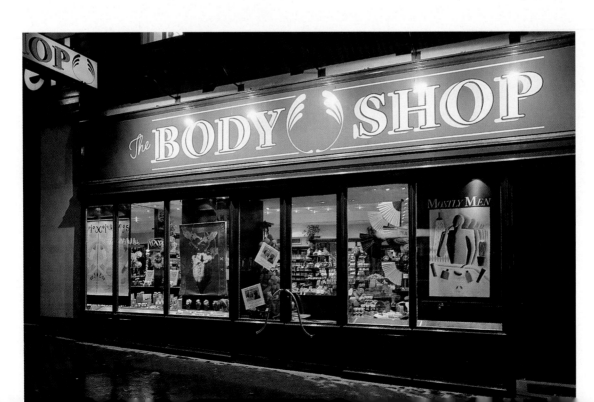

material as was used for the interior
furnishings, thus achieving a formal coherence
between the exterior and the interior.

The façade is horizontally divided into three
levels. An enormous shop sign bearing the
name and trade-mark of the chain runs the
length of the upper part of this façade. This not
only confers a unitary character, but also
ensures a much more outstanding presence in
the street. The shop sign is directly lit by a
series of lamps, attached above the sign.

The intermediate section, a glazed surface
which reaches up above head height, is divided
into equal modular sections, in such a way
that the double door blends into the
same structural unity as the different
display windows.

A green lacquered base board occupies the
bottom section of the façade the height of
which is matched, inside the shop, by raised
platforms, on which the company's most

▲ *A panoramic view of the interior.
The layout of the premises was previously broken
off into smaller areas, in the old style. The first
priority of the designer was to knock down the
partition walls which separated the space. The
result has been the creation of the present wide
open diaphanous space.*

representative products are displayed, in stark juxtaposition to other objects totally unrelated to the world of cosmetics, such as miniature cars, fans or eye-catching art posters.

The interior of this shop on Mariahifer Strasse is dominated by a well lit and diaphanous space in which, against a background of dark green and white, the products are arranged in groupings of vivid and contrasting colours. This is the image of The Body Shop, an aesthetic which, to a certain extent, we are reminded of the compositions of one of the fathers of pictorial abstraction, Piet Mondrian.

The bi-colour and rectangular backdrop acts as a contrast, allowing the sales products to acquire an added intensity. The furnishings, both in terms of the perimeter shelving and the display counters, located in the central area of the shop, provide further opportunities to highlight the exhibition of the products. These

▼ *A perspective of the main counter, with the cash register. Most of the products are directly available for the customers to serve themselves, in such a way that anyone entering the shop with the intention of buying just one product, after going round the shelves could quite easily end up buying much more*

furnishings are built of dark green varnished wood. The suspended ceiling is plastered and painted white. The flooring is laid in the form of a grid, with white and dark green stoneware tiles laid out diagonally.

What we have here is a clearly defined space which is stylishly lit by oeil-de-boeuf lamps, built into and blending with the ceiling.

The Body Shop's exclusive products are presented against this background, combined in a rich variety of still life forms, which play off the intense colouring of the products: red, green, blue, pink, ..., arranged on the shelves to recreate geometric forms. It is an abundantly vivacious image, with the fully stacked shelving units also benefiting from their back-mounted mirrors to duplicate their effect. The intention behind The Body Shop design concept is to present the purchaser with a brilliant crucible of light and colour. ■

◢ A view of the corner of the shop, with one of the beam supporting pillars, we can also appreciate that the interior design relies on some rather surprising decorative additions. In this case a chain of teddy bears hanging from the ceiling.

◀ On the previous page, a view of the central display unit, this unit has been located just below an existing cross beam, dividing the space into two independent ambiences, yet not closing them off from each other.

◄ Most of the available products can be found on the perimeter shelving units, which occupy three of the walls of the premises. A mirror has been installed just behind the shelves, giving the impression of greater width and abundance.

► A detail view of the products arranged on the shelves. The Body Shop chain specialises in both perfumery products, and also personal hygiene accoutrements.

▲ *All of the furnishings and shelving units are manufactured in beech wood varnished to a dark green colour. The ceiling is plaster finished and painted white. The flooring is a combination of white and dark green earthenware tiles, laid out in a diagonal design.*

▼ *Against the backdrop of this rectangular green and white canvas, the intense and obtrusive effect of the bright coloration of the products has a very specific effect, it is an aesthetic replete with references to the abstract expressionism of Piet Mondrian, and Theo van Doesburg.*

REGIA

Eduard Alemany

▲ *The posters and publicity photographs occupy a privileged position in the window displays, which present an extended and diaphanous image due to the sheets of plate glass which enclose them from floor to ceiling.*

▶ *Each of the window displays is centred around an elongated mirror-surfaced pyramid which supports glass shelving. The quality of the design of these display elements is, in itself, a great attraction for potential shoppers.*

▲ *The square in which the Regia perfumery is located is built on a steep slope, this aspect is exploited to full advantage in order to draw attention to the shop entrance. The projecting form of the display windows is an invitation to the passers-by to enter the space designed at the approach to the entrance doorway, thus promoting the commercial ends of the premises. The lighting is another of the factors which draws attention to this establishment.*

The perfumery Regia is situated in Plaza Pérez Cabrera, in Barcelona, on the ground floor of a brick built building designed by the architect Ricardo Bofill.

The layout of the premises is irregular, with a single exterior surface of substantial length. The entrance is at one end, slightly recessed, with the result that the display window projects out across the pavement like the prow of a ship. The square is built on a steep slope, leaving the entrance at a height considerably below that of the opposite end of the display window.

Eduard Alemany has taken full advantage of the opportunities offered by a facade of these dimensions. The display windows consist of panes of glass occupying the full height of the premises from floor to ceiling, held in place by thick frames of black lacquered steel. The name of the shop is printed in large navy blue letters on one of the windows next to the entrance.

In each of the display windows a four sided, elongated, mirror-surfaced pyramid has been placed, supporting various stepped levels of glass shelving, on which the perfumes, cosmetics products and accessories are arranged according to the different brands on display. Advertising posters, related to these products are arranged around the pyramids.

The premises are divided into two floors with completely differentiated functions. The ground floor is given over to the sale of gift articles and perfumery products, while the make-up booths occupy the first floor. The two floors are linked by an open stair well on the walls of which large advertising photographs, lit by back mounted fluorescent tubes, have been hung.

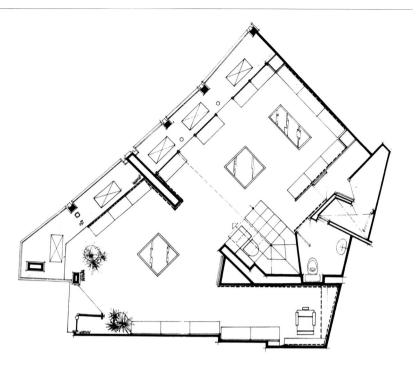

The layout of the premises is central to the creation of a variety of differentiated spaces. Although all of the shelving is mounted on the walls of the shop, the type of shelving varies depending on the area. There are also display units mounted on wheels which allow for variations in the distribution of the shop.

The flooring is of polished "San Vicens" limestone slabs. In the window displays, the flooring has been done using the same kind of stone, but here it is granular, resulting in a texture which contrasts with the smooth surfaces of the flasks and containers of the products. The lighting is by means of 50 watt dichromatic ceiling-mounted light fittings, combined with 150 watt halogen spots, giving a cold white lighting effect. ■

▲ The singularity of the emplacement of these premises constitute one of the most important inducements when it comes to defining both the exterior image and the interior distribution. The long façade of display windows benefits from the progressive slope of the pavement, creating a spectacular sequence. The asymmetric outline of the interior floor plan is taken advantage of to locate the least representative installations in corners and angles (the stairway, the washrooms), thus liberating an extensive and diaphanous central space.

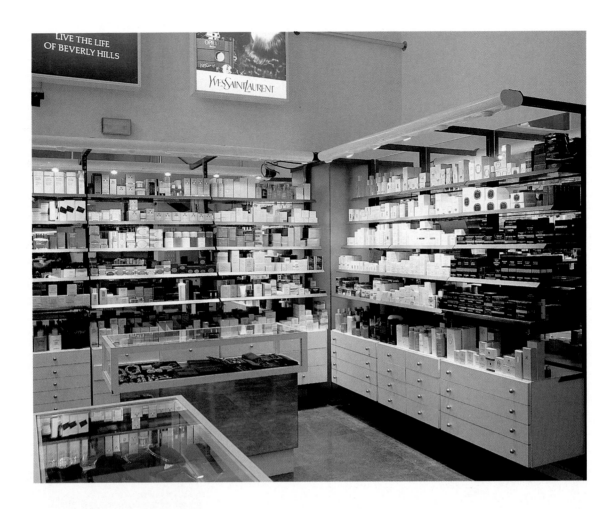

▲ The modern and functional design of the shelving units, with spots built-in to the structure allows emphasis to be placed on the products. The counters are small and discreet, with attractive mirrored front panels, reflecting the natural stone flooring. The overall impression is aseptic yet welcoming.

▲ The two floors of the perfumery are connected by a space of a double height (1). This spatial composition provides the premises as a whole with a sensation of great width, emphasising the warm base of the flooring, finished in Sant Vicens limestone slabs. The large advertising photographs provide an attractive complement to the decoration of the premises, highlighted by the fluorescent illumination.

► On the following page, one of the shop's mobile display units. Thanks to these units the products for sale are not only displayed on the shelving units which run round practically the whole of the perimeter of the shop. Their mobility and simple design allow for variations to the interior decoration and the display of products.

▶ *The irregular layout of the premises allows for the differentiation of a variety of areas. Long strings of halogen spots flood the establishment with an intense white light. Mirrors have been strategically placed in the narrow spaces to optically enlarge the shop. (3)*

◀ *Another image of the spectacular display module endows the window displays with such a singular presence. The mirrored finishing of the sides of the pyramid create an attractive interplay of reflections, and the planes of the display space fit around this almost aerial geometric design. Some of the structural elements of the building emerge in the formal composition of the window display.*

▶ *The frosted glass panels which mark off the back of the window displays also serve as shelving supports for the interior of the shop (2). The overall interior design of the shop is cold and aseptic, strengthening the highly attractive image of modernity and pragmatism. This, however, does not impede the atmosphere from being comfortable and pleasant, spacious and diaphanous. The aesthetic effectiveness of the design concedes the maximum protagonism to the customer and to the products on display.*

SAPONIFÈRE

◢ The perfumery is located in a characteristic building in the Parisian Rue Bonaparte, in Saint Germain-des-Prés, as a result of which it conserves a traditional commercial presence, in tone with the surrounding ambience.

▶ The flasks and containers also maintain this same traditional air, characteristic of the whole establishment, arranged on delicate glass shelves.

153

▲ An antique commode has been used as a display counter. This use of antique furniture, related to the style of the establishment, constitutes a functional and ornamental motif which instils confidence in a certain type of customer who find in these traditional aspects a source of security when it comes to shopping.

◀ On the previous page, a view from the entrance. The premises are long and narrow, however, the lay out of the perimeter shelving units, and a meticulous distribution of display elements. allows for the liberation of a maximum of space. The almost constant use of wood finishing contributes to the creation of a warm and welcoming atmosphere, which draws potential customers into the shop.

The Saponifère cosmetics and beauty products boutique can be found at number 59 Rue Bonaparte, in the Parisian quarter of Saint Germain-des-Prés.

Here we can find the whole range of personal hygiene products: from soaps, creams, tonics and lotions to sponges, bath robes and towels.

The layout of the premises, stretching back a long way, but with a narrow facade, was the principal conditioner of the design of both the interior and the furnishings.

The facade presents a finely balanced formal unity. Framed between two white lacquered wooden pilasters, with a wide plinth of the same material, and a dark grey awning above, it stands out as an independent element against the grey stone frontage of the building. The door is set off to one side and a single pane of glass forms the surface of the display window, to the left of the entrance. The products are arranged on a raised wooden platform. The

name and logotype of the shop are again
displayed on a half lowered sand
coloured blind.

The interior finishes are almost completely
of light coloured wood, including the floor
boards, the shelving units and the counters.
Despite the reduced dimensions of this space,
as many products as possible have been put out
on display for the customers to view. The wall
to the left is completely filled with shelving
units, angled at 45 degrees in the form of saw
teeth. This, not only results in an increase in

◄ *On the previous page, a detail view of one of the
shelving units. the products are arranged according
to their format and function, creating a series of
parallels with a pronounced aesthetic effect.*

▼ *Below, a perspective from the back of
the shop, with the commode in the
foreground, behind which there is a series of
attractively designed display cases with four
levels and golden rims.*

◄ ▼ *Some of the of the recipients showed in the Saponifère shop are handycrafts. In this example the cologne bottles.*

the shelving surface, but also adds to the visual impact of the products. The shelving units are backed by mirrored surfaces and their glass shelves are set at adjustable heights, just above the products on display, accentuating the impression of great density. Indented triangular counters have been installed, at waist height, with cupboard space beneath them.

On the opposite wall an old marble topped commode, with wooden drawers has been placed, on which a variety of personal hygiene products are displayed. On this side of the shop we again find large mirrors, interspersed with sections of ornate wall paper featuring floral motifs in earthy and ochre tones.

Adjustable spots, built into the ceiling, create a homogenous lighting effect throughout the shop. ■

▶ *The heights of the shelves can be adjusted, allowing for the display of a greater number of products. Some of the recipients showed in the Saponifère shop are handycrafts. In the example, the coloured.*